FOLDING PAPER TOYS

FOLDING
PAPER TOYS

by
Shari Lewis

AND

Lillian Oppenheimer

Scarborough House
Lanham, MD 20706

FIRST SCARBOROUGH HOUSE PAPERBACK EDITION 1993

Folding Paper Toys was originally published in hardcover by Stein and Day/Publishers.

Photos by Tony Costa
Drawings by Yukio Kondo

ISBN 0–8128–1953–5 (pbk. : alk. paper)

to

Lillian Oppenheimer

*America's beloved First Lady
of Paper Folding*

CONTENTS

About
FOLDING PAPER TOYS

N A RECENTLY RECEIVED MAIL POUCH, I found the following letter: "Dear Shari, This morning when you did paper folding on your television show, I took a piece of paper and I did what you did. You got a bird and I got a boat. What did you do wrong? (Signed) Jennie."

I didn't do anything wrong, and as I wrote and told Jennie that same day, neither did she. She had simply stumbled upon the beginnings of the classic boat fold all by herself, and once she recognized the form, she had no trouble completing the figure.

And that's the fun of folding paper toys—the excitement of knowing that around the next fold or under the hidden flap, waiting for your fingers to reveal it, lies a well-constructed, three dimensional, recognizable object with which you can play.

Origami, the art of paper folding, has become an important hobby, and many books on the subject have found their way onto the bookshelves of American homes, never to leave. In fact, these origami books seldom leave the shelves more than once because that first attempt to follow the directions reveals that the illustrations are small and complex, the instructions are confusing (often poorly translated from the Japanese), and the origami figure that you laboriously produce is hardly identifiable. And once you've decided what it is ("Turn it over—oh yes, see? It's a shrimp."), the fun is over, for most of the ancient folds in these books don't have even the smallest play value.

Mrs. Oppenheimer and I both feel that the sense of having produced a tangible and "useful" object (a boat that floats, a puppet that "talks") is very important. For a child, the incentive to pursue the instructions to the very end is often only as strong as the desire to possess the plane, noisemaker, jumping frog, or doll house that is seen in the final picture. And the fact that these dimensional origami figures are invariably beautiful is a delightful bonus.

In addition to the daily play value, the toys in this book make ideal party favors and holiday decorations. Here are just a few of the ways in which they can be used:

CHRISTMAS TREE DECORATIONS

The Flying Fish (Pg. 10) is a delicate abstract figure that will look great hanging on your tree. A fleet of sailboats (Pg. 6) sailing through a pine tree sea is sure to delight. Or decorate your tree with a family of various sized Billy Beaks (Pg. 24).

GREETING CARDS

Holiday greetings ("From our house to your house") can be written on the sides of the Doll House (Pg. 56), which can then be slipped into an envelope with ease. A charming invitation to a youngster's birthday party could be created by writing the necessary information on the sails of the Sailboat (Pg. 6).

PARTY CENTERPIECES

Place a large Doll House (Pg. 56) in the center of the table. The house has two areas to be furnished, one on each side. Make enough appropriately proportioned furniture (See pages 60 through 81) so that each child may take one piece home at the end of the party. Or use a large Sailboat in the center of the table, and maintain the boating theme by utilizing the Catamarans as candy containers and the Flying Fish as party favors. (See below.)

PARTY FAVORS

All of the flying objects, including Glider (Pg. 14), Whirlybird (Pg. 12), and the Boomerang (Pg. 18) make exciting party favors. So do the puppets Billy Beak (Pg. 24), Freddy Finger (Pg. 28) and the Frog (Pg. 32). If you think your nerves can take it, try giving the children the noisemakers—the Snapper (Pg. 46) and the Banger (Pg. 50). The Bug Catcher (Pg. 42) is a favorite because children enjoy what it can do (nose biting, fortune telling, color changing, and imaginary bug catching).

PLACE CARDS

In order to organize and supervise the seating arrangement at your party table, write each youngster's name on the sail of a tiny sailboat (Pg. 6) or the side of a miniature dollhouse (Pg. 56) or the back of a little frog (Pg. 32). Incidentally, the frog can later be used as part of a party game. (See below.)

NUT AND CANDY CONTAINERS
The twin hulls of the Catamaran (Pg. 2) provide marvelous catch-alls for party tidbits. The Bug Catcher has four separate compartments for candy. Simply turn the figure over and rest it on the four center points in order to get a bonbon dish.

PARTY GAMES
The Jumping Frog (Pg. 32) can be used competitively as a form of Tiddly Winks, with each contestant trying to "jump" his frog into a low dish or tray. The frogs can also jump for distance. The Glider (Pg. 14) lends itself to a game where the object is to see who can throw the farthest, or with the greatest accuracy (into a basket across the room). The Sailboat (Pg. 6) can be used in a table top regatta in which each child blows his ship across the table without causing it to capsize, and in the shortest amount of time.

ENTERTAINMENT
Billy Beak (Pg. 24) and Freddy Finger (Pg. 28) can joke, sing, and tell any story you can tell. The coin trick (Pg. 38) and the Bug Catcher (Pg. 42) will make a magician of you before you can say abracadabra.

MOBILES
Sailboats (Pg. 6), Flying Fish (Pg. 10), or Gliders (Pg. 14) of various sizes and colors look amusing and airy when strung in mobile form.

Toys are an expensive commodity today. I hope you will discover, as Mrs. Oppenheimer and I have, that children are oblivious to price tags. They will enjoy making and playing with paper toys, and they'll cherish those that you make for them. And you may find, as I have, that the youngsters' awed reaction to your and their accomplishments is as worthwhile as the toy itself. I was doing a show once and a little girl came over to me and said she liked the way I could make everything out of paper. I thanked her, but told her I really couldn't make everything out of paper. She wouldn't believe me. She asked me to wait right there, went away, came back two minutes later with a piece of paper, handed it to me and said very confidently, "Go ahead, Shari, there's the paper. Show me one thing, just one thing, that you can't make."

A Word from SHARI and LILLIAN

THAT INTRODUCTION WAS WRITTEN IN 1963. Since then, my little girl (Mallory, who delighted in all my early paper folding) has grown into a young woman writing books of her own and Lillian Oppenheimber, who lived to be a spry great-grandmother, has passed away. She was in her mid 90s, on the verge of seeing this book republished and still an avid "folder!"

—Shari Lewis, August 1992

Thirty years have passed since *Folding Paper Toys* was published. In 1963 Origami was a curiosity with ancient Eastern origins. Few people knew the Japanese word (*ori*—fold, *kami*—paper). I founded the Origami Center of America in my Greenwich Village brownstone in 1959 to meet the needs of the scores of new folders around the country who had discovered paper folding, but had no one with whom to share their ideas. Today, Origami is a popular international past time with millions of afficionados wherever there is paper. There are societies founded to share and spread the art in more than 30 countries. In 1978 The Friends of the Origami Center of America was founded to carry on the mission of sharing at my center. Now, as I approach my 94th birthday, The Friends has evolved into a large, generous and influential force. An all volunteer, not-for-profit arts organization with 2,000 members. The Friends welcome inquiries about its activities, regional groups and expansive supply center. Send a self-addressed envelope with 2 first-class stamps to The Friends of Origami Center of America, Box PBO, 15 West 77th Street, New York, NY 10024-5192.

—Lillian Oppenheimer, June 1992

Basic RULES OF ORIGAMI

1 | Choose a flat, hard surface as your place of work.

2 | Be sure to make your folds straight.

3 | Make your creases sharp by pressing along them with your thumbnail.

4 | If possible choose a paper with a color, texture, and design that will add beauty and interest to your model.

5 | Experiment with different kinds of paper. Try typing paper, onion skin paper, gift wrapping and shelf paper, magazine pages or covers, colored comics, and even stiff fabrics like buckram for a variety of effects.

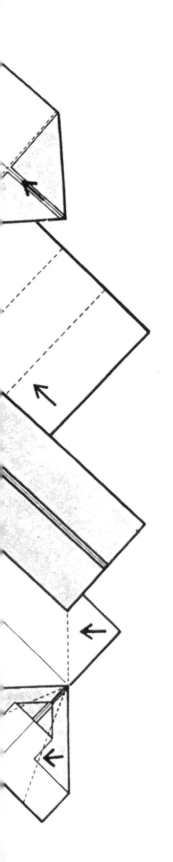

Sailing
AND
Flying
Toys

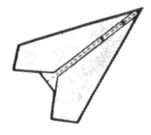

CATAMARAN

| START WITH |

A square piece of paper.

1 Bring the top edge down to meet the bottom edge, crease and open. Bring the top edge and the bottom edge together to meet the center crease. Do not open.

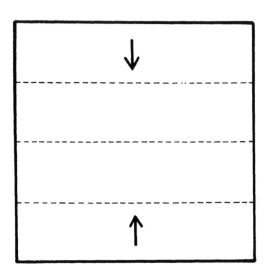

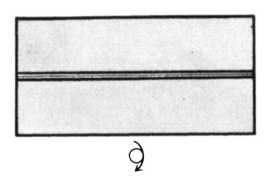

2 There are now two edges meeting in the center. Turn the paper over.

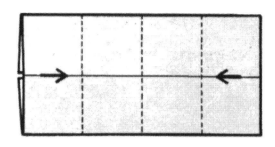

3 Bring the right edge over to meet the left edge. Crease sharply and open. Fold the right edge and the left edge in to meet the center crease. Do not open.

4 Your paper should look like this.

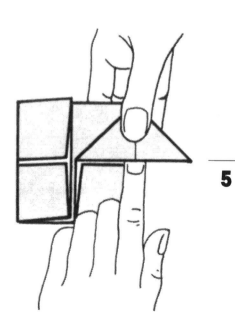

5 Hold down one square, then grasp the point of the square above it and pull it out to the side as far as it will go until that square becomes a triangle. Do the same with the other three squares. Sharpen all the creases.

CONTINUED ▶

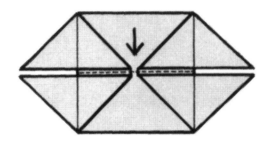

6 Fold the top edge down to meet the bottom edge.

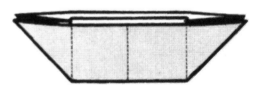

7 Stand the catamaran on its two pontoons, and it will float.

▲

CATAMARAN

SAILBOAT

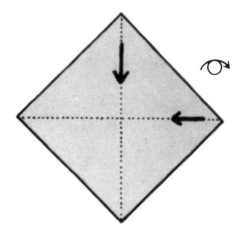

1 Bring the top point of the square down to meet the bottom point, crease sharply, and open the paper. Bring the two side points together, crease and open. Turn the paper over.

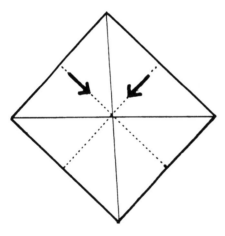

2 Bring the side edges together, crease and open. Fold the top edge to meet the bottom edge. Do not open.

3 Grasping the upper corners, push your hands together. You now have four sections.

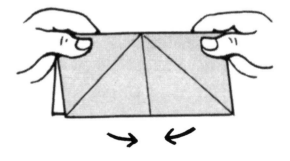

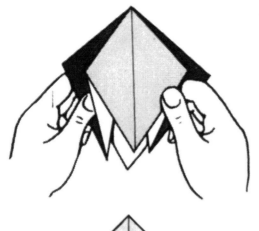

4 Flatten two of these sections on each side, forming a small square.

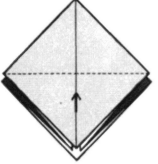

5 At the bottom point, lift the single upper layer and fold it up to meet the top point.

6 Turn the paper over.

7 Repeat step #5, lifting the bottom point of the upper single layer. Fold it to meet the top point.

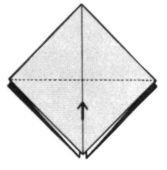

CONTINUED ▶

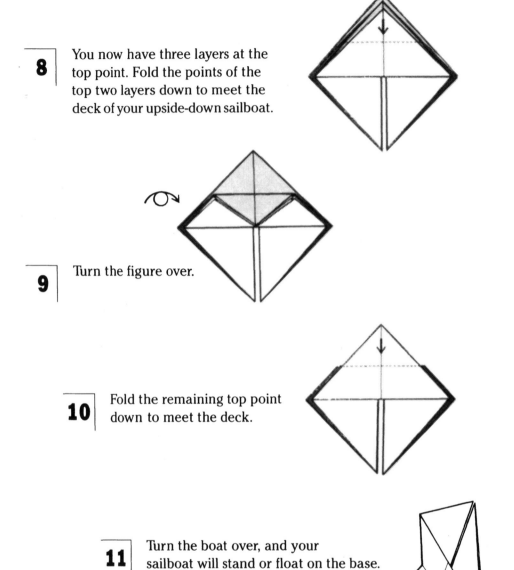

8 You now have three layers at the top point. Fold the points of the top two layers down to meet the deck of your upside-down sailboat.

9 Turn the figure over.

10 Fold the remaining top point down to meet the deck.

11 Turn the boat over, and your sailboat will stand or float on the base.

In order to give your sailboat greater stability in the water, fold only the two outer points down to make the base. This will leave the inner point to serve as a centerboard.

▲

SAILBOAT

FLYING FISH

A thin strip of thin paper.

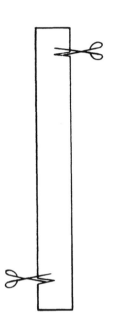

1 On the upper right hand side of the strip, cut a slit half way across the strip. Repeat on the lower left hand side of the strip.

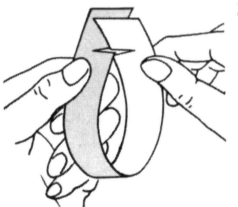

2 Bring the bottom slit up to meet the top slit and slip one into the other, linking them.

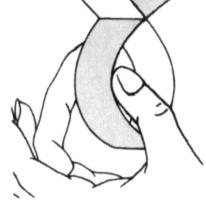

3 Throw the flying fish high into the air and it will whirl and twirl on its way to the ground.

SAILING AND FLYING TOYS

10

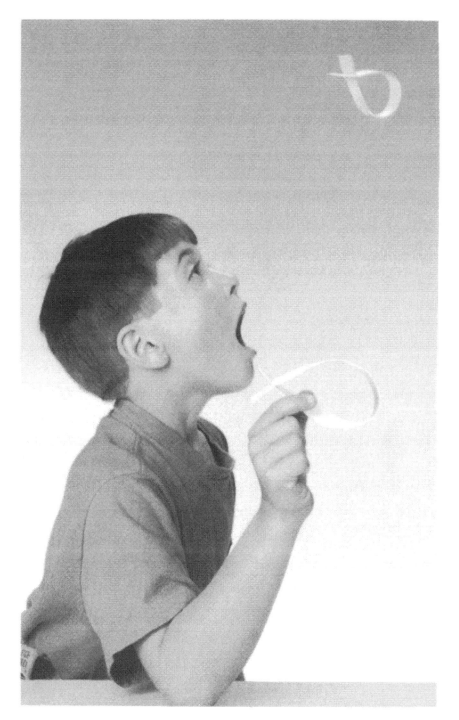

◄ FLYING
FISH

FLYING FISH

11

WHIRLYBIRD

A thin strip of paper.

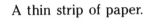

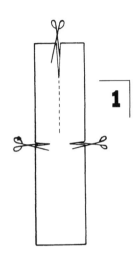

1 Make three tears or cuts in your paper. One cut is lengthwise along the center of the paper almost to the midpoint of the paper. The other two cuts are opposite one another in the midpoint of the paper, each one-third the width of the paper.

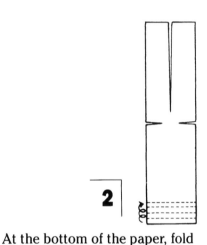

2 At the bottom of the paper, fold the bottom edge up a little, and turn this fold over on itself three times. Crease sharply.

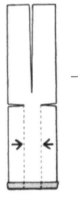

3 Fold the right edge of the lower half over as far as your cut allows. Fold the left edge of the lower half over the right side. Pick the figure up.

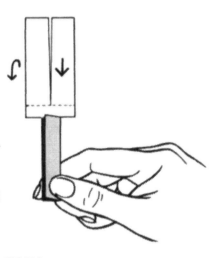

4 Fold the left upper flap away from you as far as the cut allows. Fold the right flap toward you. Throw the whirlybird high into the air and it will whirl and twirl on its way to the ground.

WHIRLYBIRD

Hold the whirlybird by the stem as high over your head as you can and let it go. By varying the length of your blades, you can make the whirlybird go faster or slower.

GLIDER

A rectangular piece of paper.
A regular 8½ x 11 sheet is ideal.

1 Fold the right edge over to meet the left edge, crease sharply, and open. Fold the right and left top corners down to meet the center crease. Do not open.

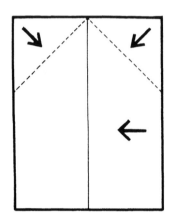

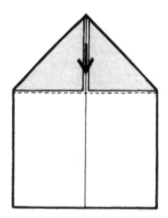

2 Fold the top triangular section down along the base of the triangle.

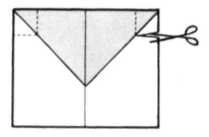

3 Cut or tear out two small equal squares at the top right and top left corners.

SAILING AND FLYING TOYS

14

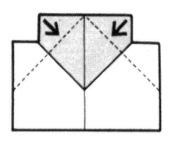

4 Fold the upper right edge down along the center crease. Do the same with the upper left edge.

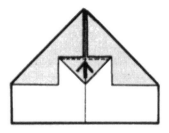

5 Fold the small triangle in the center of the paper up as far as it will go.

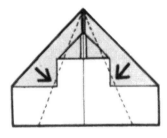

6 Fold the slanting right side over to meet the center crease. Repeat with the slanting left side.

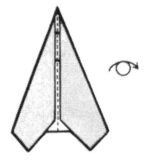

7 Turn the paper over.

CONTINUED ▶

GLIDER

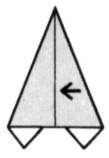

8 Fold the right half over the left half.

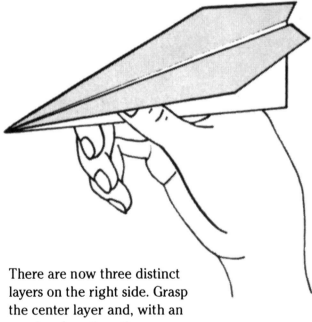

9 There are now three distinct layers on the right side. Grasp the center layer and, with an overhand motion, throw your glider.

▲

GLIDER

BOOMERANG

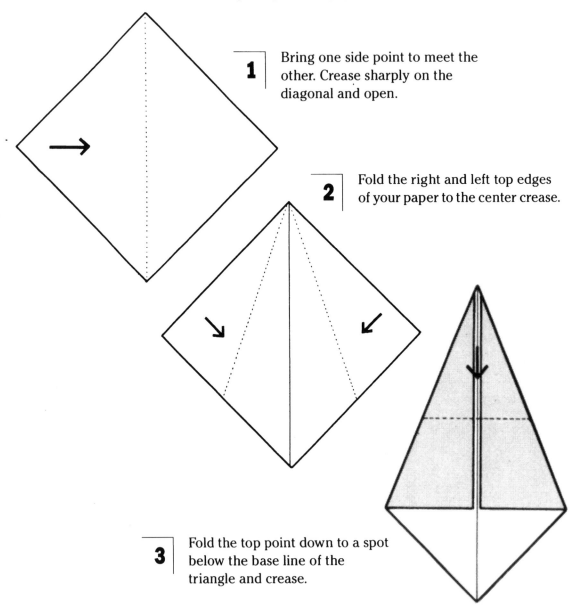

1 Bring one side point to meet the other. Crease sharply on the diagonal and open.

2 Fold the right and left top edges of your paper to the center crease.

3 Fold the top point down to a spot below the base line of the triangle and crease.

SAILING AND FLYING TOYS

18

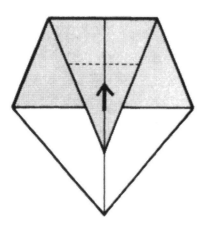

4 | Fold this point back so that it extends above the top of the paper and crease.

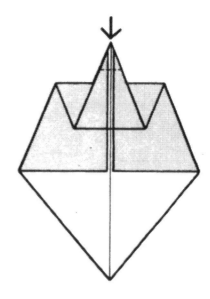

5 | Fold this point down, leaving a blunt point extending above the rest of the paper.

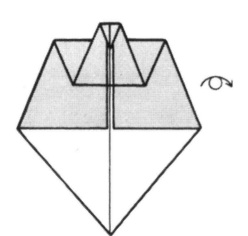

6 | Turn the paper over.

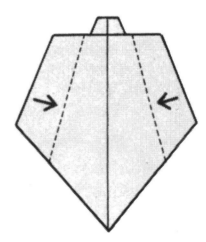

7 | Fold the right edge and the left edge of the figure in to meet the center crease.

CONTINUED ▶

BOOMERANG

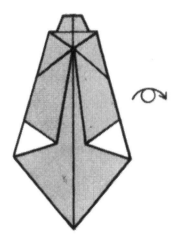 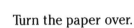 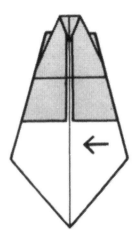

8 Turn the paper over.

9 Bring the right side of the figure over to meet the left side.

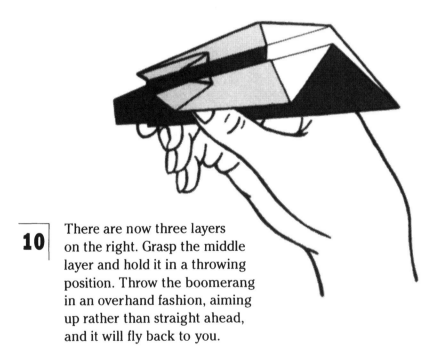

10 There are now three layers on the right. Grasp the middle layer and hold it in a throwing position. Throw the boomerang in an overhand fashion, aiming up rather than straight ahead, and it will fly back to you.

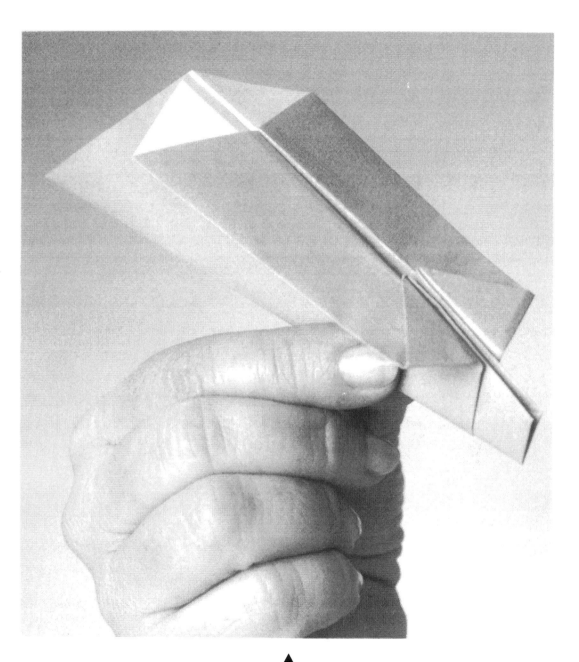

▲

BOOMERANG

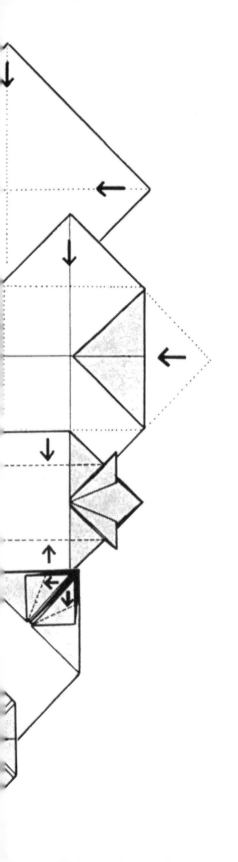

Puppets

BILLY BEAK

A square piece of paper.

1 Bring the top point down to meet the bottom point, crease the paper sharply and open it. Bring the two side points together, crease, and open it again.

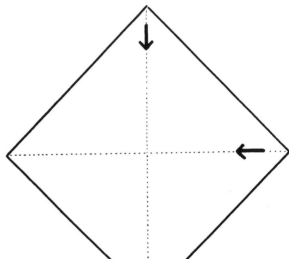

2 Now fold all four points to the center.

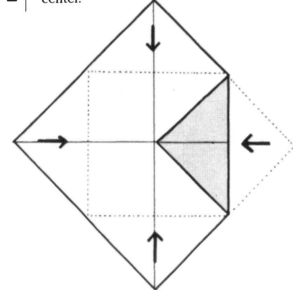

3

Turn the folded paper over.

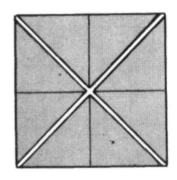

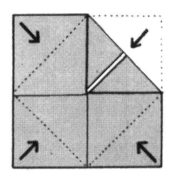

4 | Fold each of these new points to the center.

5 | Fold the bottom point up to the mid point of the square. Turn the paper over.

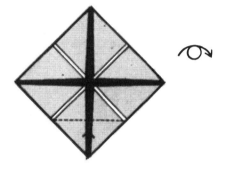

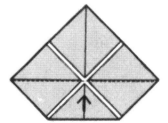

6 | Fold the lower part of the figure up along the center crease . . .

CONTINUED ▶

BILLY BEAK

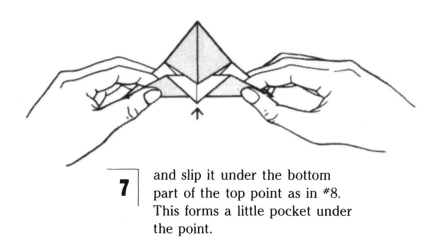

7 and slip it under the bottom part of the top point as in #8. This forms a little pocket under the point.

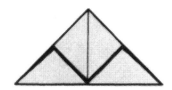

8 Fold the model back on itself through the center crease and open.

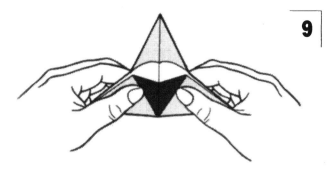

9 Press your hands gently together at the mid point of the slanting sides and pull out the little pocket to form the lower part of Billy's beak. By moving your hands together and apart Billy Beak will speak.

▲

BILLY BEAK

FREDDY FINGER

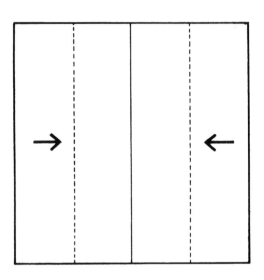

1 Bring the right edge to meet the left edge, crease sharply and open. Fold both the right edge and the left edge in to meet the center crease. Do not open.

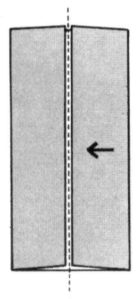

2 Now fold the right side over to meet the left side.

3 Fold the bottom edge up to meet the top edge.

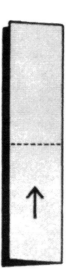

4 You now have two separate multilayered flaps. Fold all of the layers of the upper flap down to meet the bottom edge of your paper. Turn the paper over and fold the remaining flaps down.

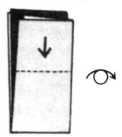

CONTINUED ▶

5 You now have two open edges and one fold between them.

6 Slip your pointer finger into the top pocket at the open end of the upper flap, and your thumb into the bottom pocket of the lower flap. Move your pointer finger up and down, and your puppet will flap his lips. (Draw the face so that his upper lip is on the top flap along the folded edge.)

▲

FREDDY FINGER

JUMPING FROG

START WITH

A 3 x 5 index card, a visiting card,
or any stiff piece of rectangular
paper of the same proportion.

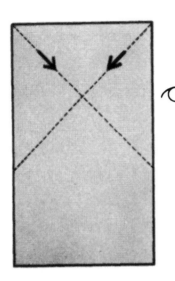

1 Fold the top edge of the paper to meet the right side of the rectangle. Crease sharply and open. Now fold the top edge to meet the left edge of the rectangle. Crease sharply and open. Turn the paper over.

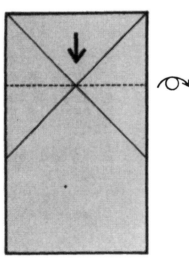

2 Fold the top edge down so that the crease runs through the center of the "X" you have created. Crease and open all the way so that the center point of the cross pops up. Turn the paper over.

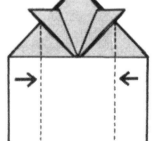

3

Push the top edge down, making sure that the right- and left-hand creases meet underneath in the center. You have now made the head and front legs of your frog.

4

Bring both the right point and the left point up to the top point, forming two flaps.

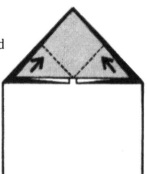

5

Fold the right flap back on itself so that the open edges lie along the folded edge beneath. Repeat with left flap.

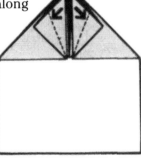

6

Fold the right edge and the left edge together to meet in the center.

CONTINUED ▶

JUMPING FROG

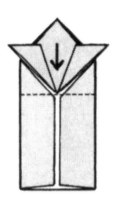

7 Fold the head and the front legs of your frog down.

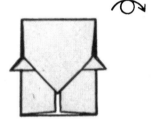

8 Turn the figure over.

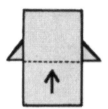

9 Fold the open bottom edge over to meet the top folded edge.

10 Turn over so that the head is away from you. By applying pressure on the back of the frog (rubbing down from nose toward the back or tapping on the back), you can make your frog jump.

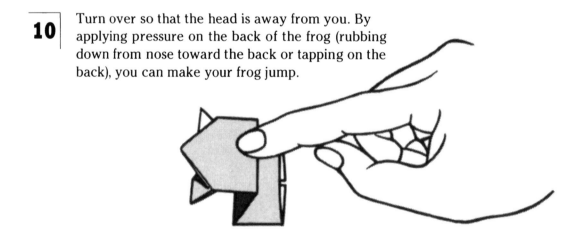

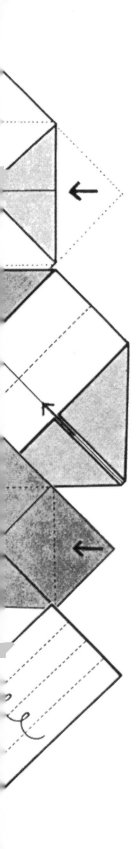

Magic
Tricks

AND

Noise
Makers

COIN TRICK

START WITH

Half of a square.

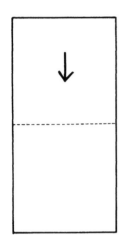

1 Fold the top half of the paper down to meet the bottom half. Crease sharply and open.

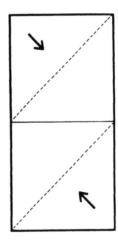

2 Fold the top edge of the paper to meet the right side of the rectangle. Fold the bottom edge to meet the left side of the rectangle.

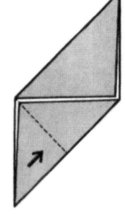

3 Fold the left double edge up to meet the center crease.

MAGIC TRICKS AND NOISE MAKERS

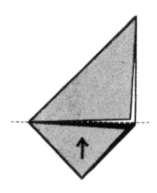

4 Fold the entire bottom triangle up along the center crease.

5 Tuck the top point all the way into the pocket of the bottom triangle as in #6.

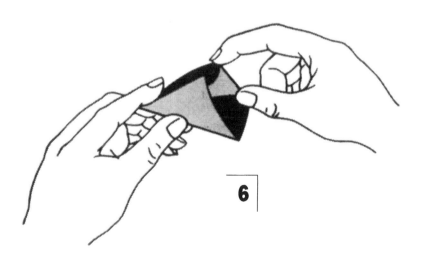

6

CONTINUED ▶

COIN TRICK

7 Crease firmly to make a flat triangle.

You are now ready to do the coin trick. The paper model has two identical pockets. Take a coin and drop it into one pocket. Turn the coin trick over and drop the coin into the palm of your hand. Do this once or twice as part of your act to set the stage for your trick. The last time leave the coin in the pocket. Pinch the pocket tightly closed. Wave the coin trick in the air several times saying appropriate magic words, then slap it flat into the palm of your other hand, at the same time turning the empty pocket toward you. Be sure to keep the pocket the coin is in closed with the palm of your hand. You can now turn the empty pocket over and the coin will seem to have disappeared. Reverse this procedure to make the coin reappear.

COIN TRICK

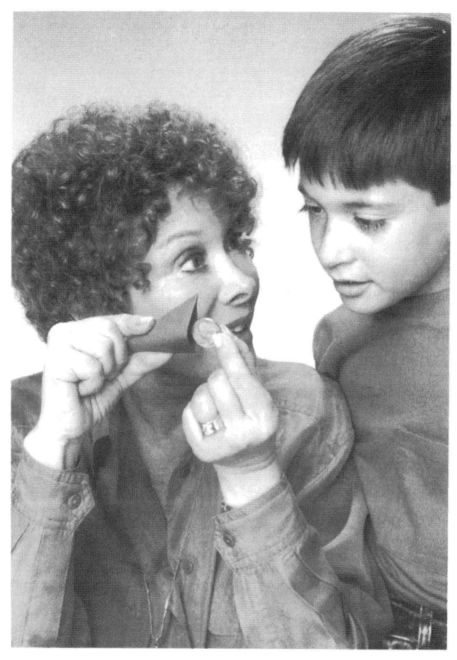

BUG CATCHER

START WITH

A square piece of paper.

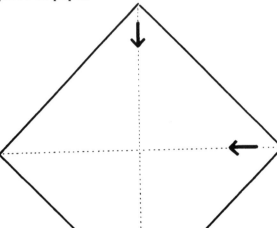

1 Bring the top point down to meet the bottom point, crease the paper sharply, and open it. Bring the two side points together, crease, and open it again.

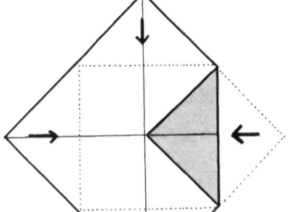

2 Now fold all four points to the center.

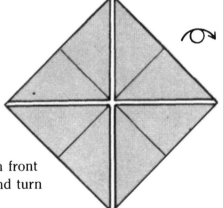

3 Place the folded paper in front of you like a diamond and turn it over.

MAGIC TRICKS AND NOISE MAKERS

42

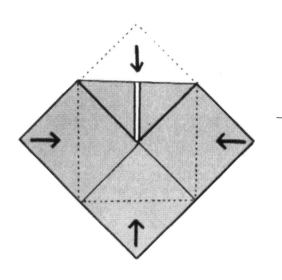

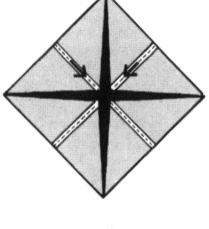

4 | Fold each of these new points to the center.

5 | Fold the right side over to the left side, crease sharply and open. Fold the top edge over the lower edge. Do not open.

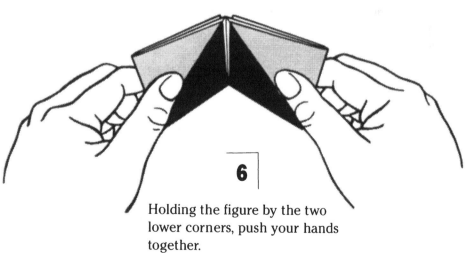

6 | Holding the figure by the two lower corners, push your hands together.

CONTINUED ▶

BUG CATCHER

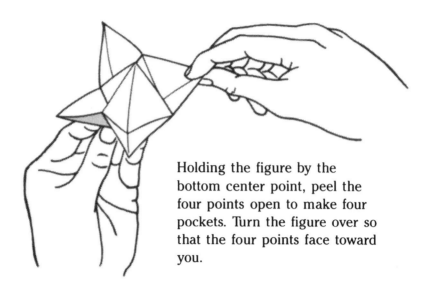

Holding the figure by the bottom center point, peel the four points open to make four pockets. Turn the figure over so that the four points face toward you.

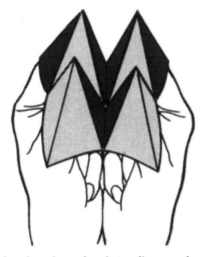

Put the thumb and pointer finger of one hand into two of the pockets, and the thumb and pointer finger of the other hand into the other two pockets. By pulling the two hands apart you get one pocket, and by pulling the two pointer fingers away from the thumbs you get another pocket.

In one of the pockets draw little bugs. By alternately showing one pocket and then the other, you can make the bugs appear and disappear. By crayoning the pockets two different colors, you can make the pocket magically seem to change color. By writing "yes" in one pocket and "no" in the other, your bug catcher can become a fortune teller and answer questions for your friends.

▲

BUG CATCHER

SNAPPER

A square piece of heavy paper.

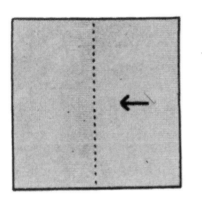

1 Fold the right edge to meet the left edge, folding the paper in half. Crease sharply.

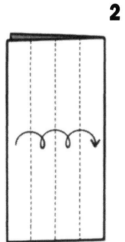

2 Lift the left side edge of the top flap and fold it over to meet the right edge. Crease and open. Bring the left edge to meet the center crease that you have just made. Do not open. Turn this flap over on itself twice to meet the right edge.

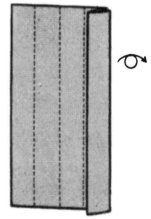

3 Turn the paper over and repeat step #2 with the right side of the paper.

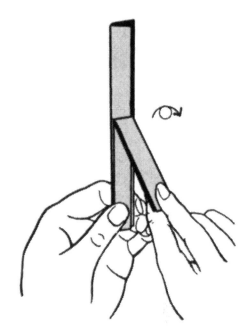

4 | Cut along the original center fold half way down your paper, creating two flaps.

5 | Fold the top edge of the top flap down as far as your cut will allow. Crease sharply. Turn the paper over and repeat with the other flap.

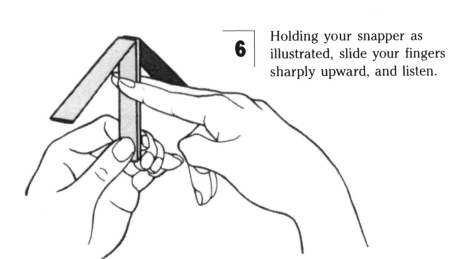

6 | Holding your snapper as illustrated, slide your fingers sharply upward, and listen.

CONTINUED ▶

SNAPPER

◀

SNAPPER

BANGER

A large rectangular piece of paper
or a sheet of newspaper.

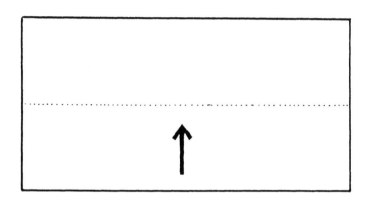

1

Bring the top edge of the
rectangle down to meet the
bottom edge. Crease sharply
and open.

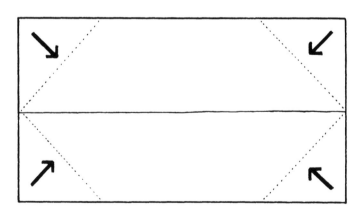

2

Fold each of the four corners in
to the center fold so that your
rectangle now comes to a sharp
point at each side.

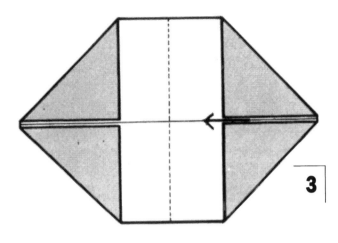

3 Fold the right point over to meet the left point. Crease sharply. Turn points toward you.

4 Lay the right half of the top fold along the center crease. Repeat with the left half of the top fold. Crease sharply, open, and turn over.

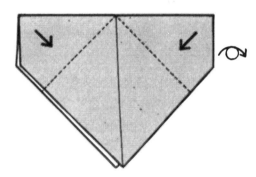

5 Once more, lay the right half and the left half of the top fold along the center crease. Crease sharply and open. (Note that you have folded along the same crease in front and back.)

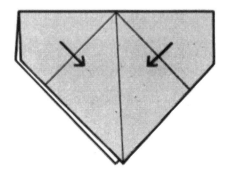

CONTINUED ▶

BANGER

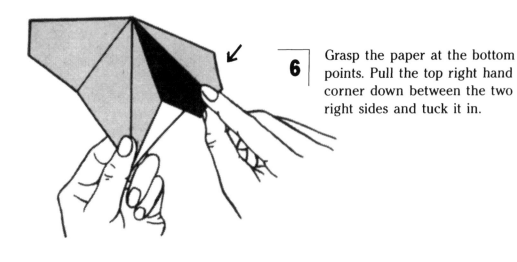

6 Grasp the paper at the bottom points. Pull the top right hand corner down between the two right sides and tuck it in.

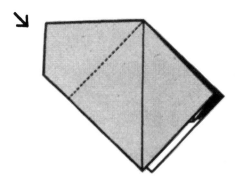

7 Pull the top left hand corner down between its two sides and tuck it in.

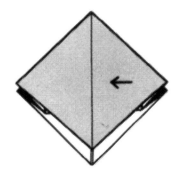

8 Fold the right points of the figure over to the left points. Sharpen all creases.

Holding your banger as illustrated, bring your arm down sharply, snapping your wrist and . . . bang!

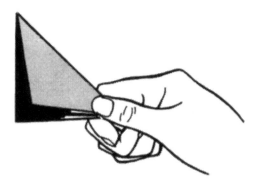

CONTINUED ▶

BANGER

BANGER

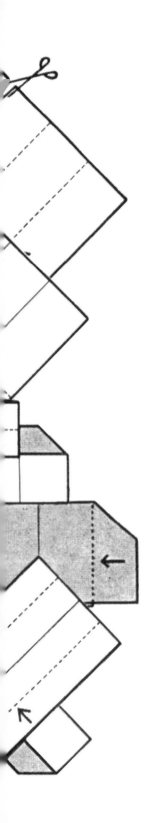

Doll
House
A N D
Furniture

HOUSE

A large square piece of paper.

1 Bring the right edge of the square to meet the left edge. Crease sharply and open the paper. Then fold the top edge down to meet the bottom edge. Crease. Do not open.

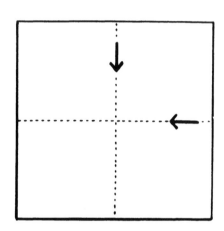

2 Fold both sides to the center crease.

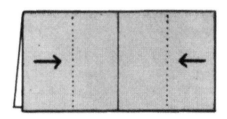

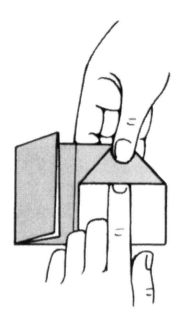

3 Lift the top layer of the right flap, insert your pointer finger and flatten the triangular "roof" that appears.

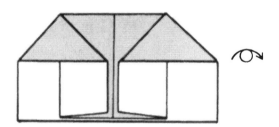

4 Repeat with left flap and turn the paper over.

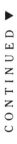

CONTINUED ▶

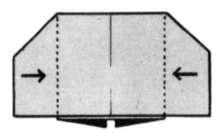

5 Fold both sides to the center crease.

6 Stand the figure upright. Gently push the four flaps out until they are standing at right angles to the center.

A roof can be placed on the house by folding a square in half and placing it across the top of the house.

▲

HOUSE

COUCH

A square piece of paper.

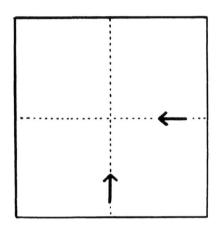

1 Bring the right edge of the square to meet the left edge. Crease sharply and open the paper. Then fold the top edge down to meet the bottom edge. Do not open.

2 Fold both sides to the center crease.

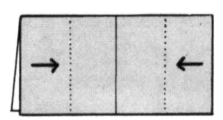

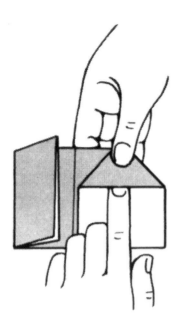

3 | Lift the top layer of the right flap, insert your pointer finger and flatten the triangular "roof" that appears.

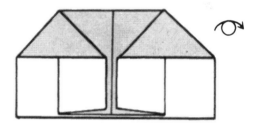

4 | Repeat with the left flap.

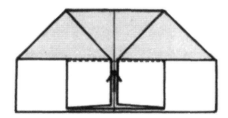

5 | Fold the bottom edge of the center panel up to meet the top edge of the figure.

CONTINUED ▶

COUCH

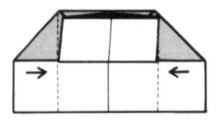

6 Fold both sides to the center crease as in #7.

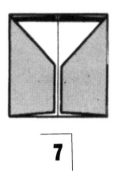

7

8 Encircle the sides of the figure with the fingers of one hand. With the other hand, pull the center panel down until it forms a seat.

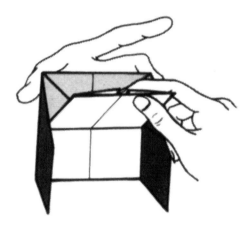

DOLL HOUSE AND FURNITURE

▲

COUCH

BUREAU

```
┌─────────────────────────┐
│      START WITH         │
└─────────────────────────┘
```

A square piece of paper.

Follow instructions for Couch (Pg. 60) from #1–8.

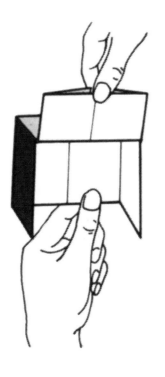

9 With one hand, grasp the back of the couch at the base. With the other hand, grasp the seat and pull it up until the seat of the couch has become the "standing mirror" of the bureau. Your bureau is now facing away from you. (A piece of silver foil pasted onto the front of the "mirror" will enhance the illusion.)

Bed

START BY

Making two couches out of two equal squares.
The mattress is made from a third square of the same size.

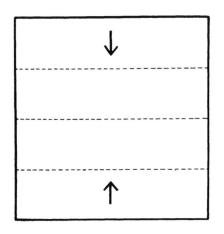

1 Bring the bottom edge of the square to meet the top edge. Crease sharply and open the paper. Then fold both the top edge and the bottom edge to the center crease. Do not open.

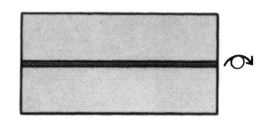

2 Turn the paper over.

3

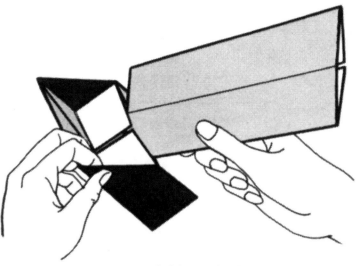

Slip one open end of the mattress into the pocket in the seat of the sofa. You now have two pillows at the head of the bed. Now slip the entire seat of the other couch into the pocket formed by the other open end of the mattress.

DOLL HOUSE AND FURNITURE

▲

BED

PIANO

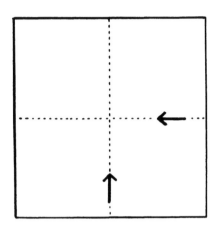

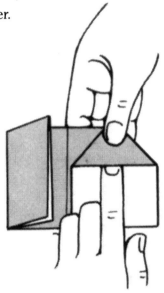

1 Bring the right edge of the square to meet the left edge. Crease sharply and open the paper. Then fold the top edge down to meet the bottom edge. Do not open.

3 Lift the top layer of the right flap, insert your pointer finger and flatten the triangular "roof" that appears.

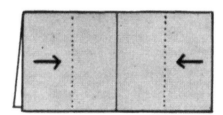

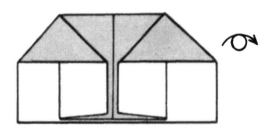

2 Fold both sides to the center crease.

4 Repeat with the left flap, and turn the paper over.

DOLL HOUSE AND FURNITURE

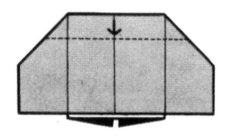

5 Fold the top of the piano down a bit.

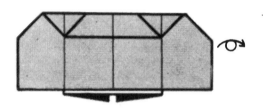

6 Turn model over.

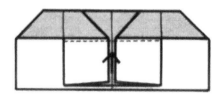

7 Fold the bottom edge of the center panel up as far as it will go.

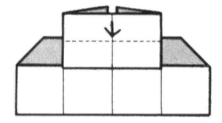

8 Now fold the top edge of this panel down in half.

CONTINUED ▶

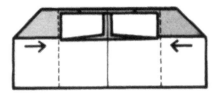

9 | Fold both side edges to the center crease as in #10.

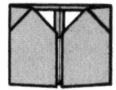

10

11 | Encircle the figure with the fingers of one hand, and with the other hand, grasp the open edges of the center panel and pull down to form the keyboard.

DOLL HOUSE AND FURNITURE

▲

PIANO

PIANO BENCH

START WITH

Half of a square of paper.

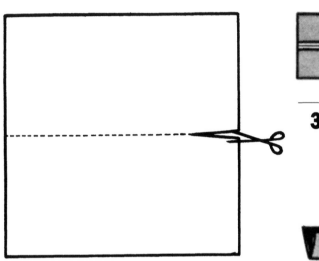

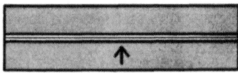

3 Fold the bottom edge of the figure to meet the top edge. Crease sharply.

1 Bring the bottom edge of the rectangle up to meet the top edge. Crease sharply and open the paper.

4 Fold the two side edges toward the center and crease sharply.

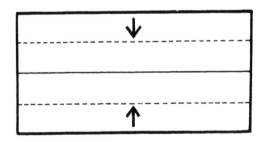

2 Now fold both the top edge and the bottom edge to the center crease. Do not open.

5 Raise these flaps up to form the legs of your bench and set it in an upright position.

▲

PIANO BENCH

TABLE

A square piece of paper.
By varying the size of the square,
you can make either a coffee table or a dining table.

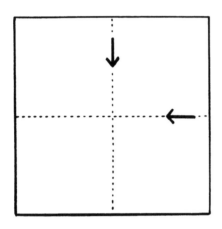

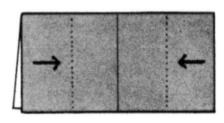

2 Fold both sides to the center crease.

1 Bring the right edge of the square to meet the left edge. Crease sharply and open the paper. Then fold the top edge down to meet the bottom edge. Do not open.

3 Lift the top layer of the right flap, insert your pointer finger and flatten the triangular "roof" that appears.

DOLL HOUSE AND FURNITURE

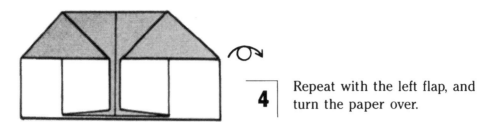

4 | Repeat with the left flap, and turn the paper over.

5 | Fold both sides to the center crease.

6 | At the bottom of the paper there are two distinct layers. Lift the upper layer only, and fold the bottom edge of this layer up to meet the top edge of the figure.

CONTINUED ▶

TABLE

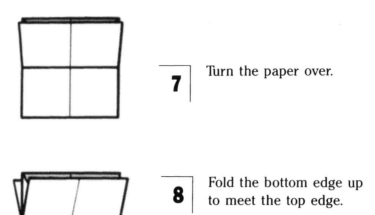

7 Turn the paper over.

8 Fold the bottom edge up to meet the top edge.

With another piece of paper of the same size, repeat steps #1–8. You now have the two halves of the table.

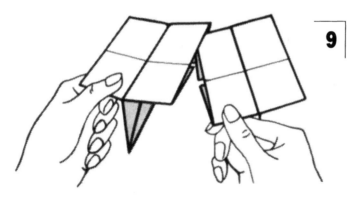

9 To put them together, hold both figures so that the closed center panel on each is pointing down. Slip the open side flap of one of the figures into the pocket formed by the open side flap of the other figure. (For a drop-leaf table, fold the remaining flaps down.)

▲

TABLE

CHAIR

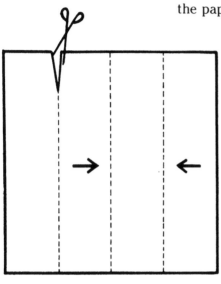

1 Bring the right edge of the square to meet the left edge, crease sharply and open the paper. Then fold both sides to the center crease and open the paper. Cut or tear off one of the end panels (or one-quarter of the paper).

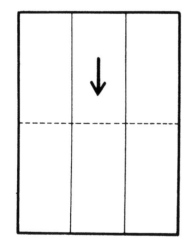

2 Fold the top edge of the paper down to meet the bottom edge. Crease sharply. Do not open.

3 Fold the right side to meet the crease on the left side.

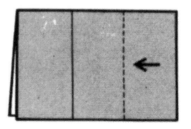

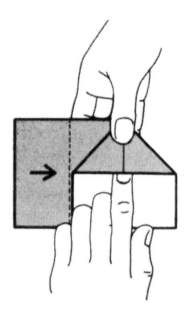

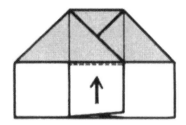

4 Lift the top layer of the right flap, insert your pointer finger and flatten the triangular "roof" that appears. Fold the left side over to cover half of the "roof."

5 Lift the top layer of the left panel, insert your pointer finger (as in #4) and flatten the triangular "roof" that appears. Then fold the bottom edge of the center panel up to meet the top edge of the figure.

CONTINUED ▶

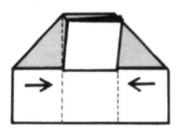

6 | Fold the left side over the center panel and then fold the right side over the left panel as in #7. Crease sharply.

7

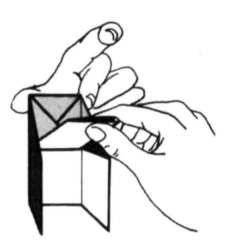

8 | Encircle the sides of the figure with one hand. With the other hand, pull the center panel down until it forms a seat.

▲

CHAIR

BIBLIOGRAPHY

If you enjoy origami, you may want to look for more books on paper-folding. This list represents only a sample of the many wonderful books available. It concentrates on those particularly suitable for the beginning folder.

Complete Origami, Eric Kenneway, St. Martin's Press, 1987, New York. An encyclopedia of origami; very informative with beautiful photographs and interesting models to inspire you. (Simple to Complex)

Decorative Napkin Folding for Beginners and *More Decorative Napkin Folding,* Lillian Oppenheimer and Natalie Epstein, Dover Publications, 1979 and 1984, New York. Clear drawings and instructions for folding napkins into ingenious and beautiful forms. (Simple)

Folding Paper Puppets, Shari Lewis and Lillian Oppenheimer, Scarborough House, 1962, New York. (New edition due Spring 1993). This book describes how to make animated puppets that actually work; a bird that flaps its wings, a fish with a moving mouth, and other origami figures with play value. Detailed illustrations take the reader from the first fold to the last. It is of special value in introducing children to paperfolding. (Simple)

The Joy of Origami, Toshie Takahama, Japan Publications, 1985, Tokyo. A lovely combination of traditional and original origami models presented in clear drawings with minimal text. (Simple to Intermediate)

The Magic of Origami, Alice Gray and Kunihiko Kasahara, Japan Publications, 1977, Tokyo. A collection of delightful and clever models, clearly diagrammed, with helpful hints throughout. The beginning of the book provides an excellent introduction to the basics of origami; the back features a large selection of holiday models and ideas for using them as ornaments. (Simple to Intermediate)

Origami, Hideaki Sakata, Graph-Sha Ltd., 1984, Tokyo. Traditional models taught from color photographs. (Simple to Intermediate)

Origami: New Ideas for Paperfolding, Gay Merrill Gross, Mallard Press, 1990, New York. The beauty and practicality of origami is emphasized in this colorful and elegantly-designed book. Very clear drawings and text give instructions for making a variety of toys, flowers, jewelry, stationery and containers. The book also gives information on creating your own patterned papers and other techniques related to origami. (Simple to Intermediate).

Paper Pandas and Jumping Frogs, Florence Temko, China Books, 1986, San Francisco. Clear drawings and text provide an introduction to origami for the younger folder. Ideas for using your folded figures are included, as well as information on the history of paperfolding. (Simple)

Wings & Things: Origami That Flies, Stephen Weiss, St. Martin's Press, 1984, New York. Along with the familiar paper airplane, this book offers the intermediate folder an assortment of novel ideas for flying models: a Flying Nun, a Gliding Swan, a Flying Bat, Dollar Bill Gliders, and many others. The text is well-written and the diagrams are clearly drawn. (Intermediate)